Original title: 101 STRANGE BUT TRUE MOTOGP FACTS

©101 STRANGE BUT TRUE MOTOGP FACTS,
Carlos Martínez Cerdá y Víctor Martínez Cerdá, 2023

© Cover and illustrations: V&C Brothers Proofreading: V&C Brothers

Writers: Víctor Martínez Cerdá and Carlos Martínez Cerdá (V&C Brothers)

Layout and design: V&C Brothers

All rights reserved. No part of this publication may be reproduced, stored in a retrieval system or transmitted in any form or by any means, mechanical, photochemical, electronic, magnetic, electro-optical, photocopying, information retrieval system, or otherwise, now or in the future, without the prior written permission of the copyright holders.

101 STRANGE BUT TRUE MOTOGP FACTS

INCREDIBLE AND SURPRISING EVENTS

1

In 1949, the International Motorcycling Federation (FIM) created the World Championship, organizing its first edition in that year.

Since then, the different categories have varied.

In fact, the 50cc category has even remained for a time.

Until 2002, the premier category was called 500cc, but it was renamed to the current name to give it more punch, and the engine capacity was increased to 990cc with 4-stroke motorcycles.

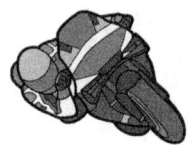

2

The suit that riders wear to get on their motorcycles must provide them with lightness to carry out the maneuvers required by the different tracks of the championship, as well as resistance to possible falls they may suffer.

In fact, when this happens, their protections remain in place and stop the abrasion that can destroy them completely, all of which prevents serious consequences for the physical integrity of the riders.

They weigh around four and a half kilos, and two materials are usually used for their making: cowhide and kangaroo leather.

Finally, they have a ventilation system integrated with holes in the front and rear areas.

3

Riders suffer from the heat and effort they have to make in each race of the championship.

They lose between 2 and 3% of their total body weight, which is equivalent to a range of one and a half to two kilos.

And it is not uncommon for tracks to exceed 35 degrees, which means an additional burden in terms of ventilation and cooling for the participants.

This circumstance highlights the importance of hydration so that they can focus on the entire race and not be distracted by environmental conditions.

4

8-time world champion Marc Márquez sports an ant on his helmet as his icon and brand image.

The origin of this can be traced back to the early years he competed in circuits, specifically when he did it in the Spanish Speed Championship (CEV).

The rider from Cervera was very light due to his small stature, which was a disadvantage for him.

As a solution, his team provided him with an additional weight of 21 kilos, which made him race for several seasons carrying twice his weight, similar to what this insect does when carrying food that is 50 times its weight.

5

In circuits like Losail (Qatar), the consumption of alcoholic beverages is prohibited due to the Muslim culture of the country.

Therefore, in the podium celebrations that take place after each race, the top 3 finishers drink a similar carbonated beverage, as if it were non-alcoholic champagne, to celebrate their great result.

This is called Waard and, they say, has an identical taste to fruit juice.

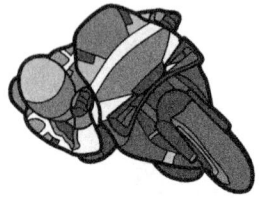

6

The use of legs in corners is an interesting topic in MotoGP, as riders use it in various ways.

Some use it to help lean the bike into the corner and maintain stability, while others use it to maintain body position and improve aerodynamics on the exit of the corner.

As for the use of boots for braking, it is true that the sole of the boots is not designed to withstand friction with the asphalt.

In addition, the brakes of competition bikes are very powerful and riders need great precision and sensitivity to apply them correctly, something that is easier to achieve with fingers than with the sole of the boot.

In summary, the use of legs and boots in MotoGP is a matter of personal preference and driving style, and each rider has their own technique to maximize the performance of their bike in each corner.

7

The act of sticking out the knee in corners is a widely used technique by MotoGP riders.

This is because by doing so, they gain greater control over the bike, as they can better measure the angle of inclination and the movement of their body helps to balance the bike and maintain grip in the corners.

Additionally, it allows them to reduce air resistance and improve aerodynamics, which can be crucial for gaining a few tenths of a second and improving speed on straights.

Although sticking out the knee may seem like a dangerous maneuver, riders train intensely to master this technique and minimize risks.

For this, they perform specific balance and coordination exercises, as well as practices on training circuits where they can simulate the situations they will encounter in races.

Additionally, they use special competition suits that have knee protections to avoid injuries in case of a fall.

8

The mobile clinic is a medical service that was implemented in MotoGP starting from the 1977 season.

It is a mobile medical team that accompanies the riders in every race to provide immediate medical attention in case of accidents or injuries.

The first rider who needed the attention of the mobile clinic was Franco Uncini, during the Austrian Grand Prix in the 350 cc category.

The mobile clinic is composed of a team of doctors and nurses specialized in traumatology and emergency care.

Additionally, it has a medicalized helicopter to quickly transport riders to a hospital if necessary.

This service has been essential to guarantee the safety of the riders and has constantly evolved over the years to improve the quality of medical care in the MotoGP sport.

9

The top speed record is 362.4 kilometers per hour.

Frenchman Johan Zarco and Australian Brad Binder share the top speed record on a MotoGP bike, as well as the fact that they both achieved it in the same year: 2021.

The Ducati Pramac rider set the record in the FP4 of the opening race at the Losail circuit, aided by the long main straight.

The KTM rider also took advantage of the length of the Mugello straight to match the record of the rider from the Borgo Panigale satellite team in the FP3 of the Italian Grand Prix.

10

The 2017 season was one of the most accident-prone in MotoGP history in terms of crashes.

A total of 1,126 crashes were recorded across the three categories, MotoGP, Moto2, and Moto3.

The majority of the crashes occurred in the Moto2 category, with a total of 434 crashes, followed by Moto3 with 379 crashes and MotoGP with 313 crashes.

This statistic was a concern for many riders and teams, as crashes can put the riders' health at risk and can also affect the performance of the motorcycles and their ability to compete in future races.

Crashes can also have an impact on the final championship standings, as points are awarded based on the riders' performance in each race.

However, measures have since been taken to improve safety on the track and reduce the number of crashes in MotoGP.

These measures include improvements in tires, suspension and brake systems, and the implementation of new traction and stability control technologies.

11

In the past, an additional point was also awarded in the MotoGP category to the rider who achieved the fastest lap in the race, as long as they finished in the points-scoring zone.

This rule was applied at different times and with various variations.

Currently, the rule of an extra point for the fastest lap in MotoGP has been in effect since the 2019 season.

Similar to Formula 1, an extra point is awarded to the rider who achieves the fastest lap in the race as long as they finish in the points-scoring zone.

Regarding past rules, in the early seasons of the Motorcycle World Championship, only the top five finishers scored points, so the winner was awarded 10 points.

Starting in 1969, points were awarded to the top six finishers.

In 1977, the rule of an extra point for the fastest lap in the race was introduced, but it only applied if the rider who achieved it finished on the podium.

In 1988, the rule changed so that the extra point was awarded if the rider who achieved the fastest lap finished in the points-scoring zone, as it is today.

In the 1990s, the rule of an extra point for the fastest lap in MotoGP was absent for some years but returned in 2003.

Since then, it has remained in effect in different formats. In some seasons, the extra point was awarded only if the rider who achieved the fastest lap finished on the podium.

In others, the current rule of awarding the extra point if the rider finished in the points-scoring zone was applied.

12

The MotoGP World Championship was established in 1949, although at that time it was known as the World Championship of Speed.

During the early years of the championship, the organizational structure was much less sophisticated than it is today, and the race calendar was much smaller.

In the first season of 1949, only six races were held, all in Europe.

The following season, in 1950, also consisted of six races, and only the three best results of each rider were taken into account for the overall standings, which meant that riders only had to participate in a limited number of races to have a chance of winning the championship.

At that time, motorcycle races were held on public roads closed to traffic, which posed a significant safety challenge for riders.

However, this also added a sense of adventure and excitement to the races, and the races became a popular event throughout Europe.

13

The airbag is in the racing suits, although it doesn't act exactly like in a passenger car since the morphology of the vehicle is different.

In any case, it automatically deploys after a crash to protect the rider's ribs, collarbones, and torso.

It is a kind of vest that inflates and, for that to happen, it needs an expansion of the suit of between 4 and 5 centimeters in the area where the airbags are located.

It takes just 25 milliseconds to deploy, 14 times faster than the human eye blinks.

To achieve this, it is connected to calibrated gyroscopes and accelerometers.

14

Nowadays, MotoGP bikes are equipped with a large number of sensors and electronic devices that gather information about the bike and the rider's performance during the race.

This data is stored on the bike's hard drive and downloaded at the end of the race for analysis.

However, during the race, teams cannot access this information to make real-time decisions that could change the course of the race.

In fact, it is prohibited by the MotoGP regulations for teams to communicate with riders during the race to provide information or strategies.

This prohibition is established to ensure that the race is as fair and exciting as possible, and to prevent teams from manipulating race results through communication with riders.

Instead, riders must rely on their own instincts and information they can gather from the track and the bike during the race.

After the race, teams can analyze the data collected by the bike's sensors and electronic devices to improve its performance and make adjustments for the next race.

This allows teams and riders to improve their performance and gain a competitive advantage over their rivals.

15

The official Honda team in MotoGP is one of the most successful teams in the category.

Known as Repsol Honda, they have won numerous championships and races over the years.

During some seasons, the Repsol Honda team had a quartet of riders, which was quite unusual in the world of motorcycle racing.

The first rider to be part of this quartet was Australian Mick Doohan, who won five consecutive MotoGP titles between 1994 and 1998.

In the 1996 season, the Repsol Honda team added Japanese rider Shinichi Ito to their lineup, who had won the 250cc World Championship in 1993.

The following year, the team recruited Japanese rider Takuma Aoki, who had won the 125cc World Championship in 1995.

In the 1998 season, the Repsol Honda team added Spanish rider Sete Gibernau to their lineup, who had competed in the 250cc category for several seasons.

Gibernau remained with the team for two seasons and achieved his first MotoGP victory in 2001.

Spanish rider Álex Crivillé also formed part of the Repsol Honda team for several seasons, winning the MotoGP World Championship in 1999.

Tadayuki Okada also competed for the team in several seasons and achieved several victories in the 500cc category.

Although the quartet of Repsol Honda riders was a rarity in the world of motorcycle racing, the team achieved great success with these riders, winning several MotoGP World Championships and races.

16

Marc and Álex Márquez are two Spanish brothers who have had a great career in the world of motorcycle racing.

Marc Márquez is a highly successful MotoGP rider who has won several world titles, while Álex Márquez has competed in various categories and has won titles in Moto3 and Moto2.

One of the interesting things the Márquez brothers share is that they have achieved victories on the same day and have been crowned world champions in the same year on several occasions.

This happened for the first time at the Catalan and Dutch Grand Prix in 2014, when Marc won the MotoGP race and Álex won the Moto3 race on the same day.

In addition, both brothers were crowned world champions in their respective categories that same year, with Marc winning the MotoGP championship and Álex winning the Moto3 championship.

The second time the Márquez brothers achieved this feat was at the French Grand Prix in 2019, when Marc won the MotoGP race and Álex won the Moto2 race on the same day.

On this occasion, both brothers were also crowned world champions in their respective categories at the end of the season, with Marc winning the MotoGP championship and Álex winning the Moto2 championship.

These coincidences are very rare in the world of motorcycle racing, and it is a testament to the talent and dedication of the Márquez brothers.

Both have had successful careers and continue to compete in the world of motorcycle racing.

17

Currently, the premier class of MotoGP uses four-stroke motorcycles with a maximum displacement of 1000cc.

These engines are highly sophisticated and are built with advanced materials, such as titanium alloys and other lightweight metals, and feature advanced electronic management technologies.

The displacement limit has varied throughout the history of the MotoGP championship, with maximum displacements ranging from 500cc to 1000cc.

The premier class changed to the current displacement of 1000cc in 2012, replacing the previous maximum displacement of 800cc.

The power of MotoGP engines has significantly increased in recent years, exceeding 270 horsepower in some motorcycles.

The top speed of these bikes varies depending on the circuit, but typically exceeds 300 km/h on long straights.

In addition, MotoGP motorcycles feature advanced suspension, braking, and tire technologies specifically designed to provide optimal performance on high-speed circuits and tight corners.

All of this makes MotoGP bikes one of the most advanced and exciting racing machines in the world.

18

Honda and Yamaha have dominated the premier class of MotoGP since the category was renamed in 2002.

In fact, both brands have won every constructor championship in that category, except for three occasions.

In 2007, Casey Stoner won the championship on a Ducati, breaking Honda's streak of 5 consecutive titles.

And in the 2020 and 2021 seasons, Andrea Dovizioso and Joan Mir, respectively, managed to bring Ducati and Suzuki to the top of the constructor championship, thus interrupting the dominance of Honda and Yamaha.

However, despite these results, Honda and Yamaha remain the most successful brands in MotoGP history, with a total of 29 and 22 constructor titles respectively.

19

Fabio Quartararo is a French motorcycle racer born on April 20, 1999 in Nice.

He began racing at the age of four and became the European Moto3 champion in 2013 and Moto2 champion in 2018.

In 2019, he made his debut in the MotoGP category and in 2020 he joined the official Yamaha team, where he won his first premier class championship title in 2021.

The nickname "The Devil" arose in his childhood because his father placed a sticker with the cartoon character's image on his racing helmet.

From there, everyone started calling him that and he adopted it as his nickname on the tracks.

Even today, he wears an image of the character on his helmet and racing gear.

20

MotoGP riders have personalized training routines, as each one has different physical needs depending on their height, weight, and the type of bike they use.

Some of the taller riders, like Aleix Espargaró, usually focus on cycling, as this activity helps improve cardiovascular and muscular endurance, as well as coordination and balance.

Other riders, like Marc Márquez and Johann Zarco, who are shorter in stature, prefer to train in the gym to strengthen the muscles they use on the bike and improve their overall physical endurance.

In addition, many riders practice additional sports that help them improve in different aspects, such as climbing to improve strength and endurance, skiing to work on balance and coordination, or even water sports like surfing or kitesurfing to improve concentration and adaptability to changing situations.

All of this is complemented by a balanced diet and adequate rest to recover the body after training and races.

21

The death of Daijiro Kato in the opening race of 2003 was a shock to the paddock and fans of this sport.

The Japanese rider suffered a spectacular crash when his Honda hit the barriers at a speed of over 200 kilometers per hour.

At 26 years old, he was on his way to becoming one of the great references in the premier class, an exceptional talent who had been the champion of the 250 cubic centimeters category.

The organization pointed to the precarious safety conditions of the Japanese circuit as one of the reasons that caused his death.

Since this sad event, racing has not returned to this track.

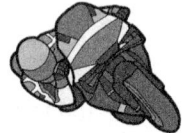

22

It is not very common to see a crash in which the rider has to jump off the bike to avoid further harm, but that is what happened to Maverick Viñales during the 2020 Austrian Grand Prix.

The Spanish rider, who was then riding for Yamaha, ran out of brakes and had been running in that difficult situation for several laps since he later admitted that he felt they were not working properly from the fourth lap onwards.

Going at over 200 kilometers per hour, he jumped off the bike as best he could and let it run into the gravel until it collided heavily with the barriers and caught fire.

Perhaps he lost the opportunity to score some valuable points for that fiercely contested championship, but he gained an extra life that will allow him to enjoy more moments with his loved ones and years of sports career ahead.

23

A spine-chilling moment was experienced during the MotoGP race at the 2020 Austrian Grand Prix at the Spielberg circuit, a week before what happened to Viñales.

French rider Johann Zarco and Italian-Brazilian Franco Morbidelli were the protagonists.

The Ducati rider tried to overtake him at the end of turn 3 by trying to brake late, but he made the mistake of braking suddenly, causing the Yamaha rider to hit him without practically any reaction time.

As a result, the Yamaha went straight while the Ducati shot towards the circuit barriers, spinning in the air, and miraculously did not collide with Valentino Rossi or Maverick Viñales, who were riding just ahead.

Tragedy was narrowly avoided, but fortunately both riders were able to tell the tale.

24

The crash suffered by Jorge Lorenzo, Dani Pedrosa, and Andrea Dovizioso during the Jerez race in 2018 caused a lot of talk.

With 8 laps to go, the Honda rider tried to overtake the two Ducatis on the inside of turn 6, which is preceded by a long straight.

Number 26 saw enough room to gain two positions and take advantage of the fight the red riders were having, but Lorenzo closed the door on him as he exited the turn, causing him to fall and take his teammate down as well.

Marc Márquez seized the opportunity and won the race, taking a significant step towards his seventh world title.

25

Jorge Lorenzo – China 2008.

The Spanish rider was plagued by crashes throughout his MotoGP career, suffering them in all shapes and sizes during his 12 seasons in the championship.

However, it must be said to his credit that he knew how to bounce back from some of them in a big way.

An example was the one he had in his debut year, 2008, during the first free practice session of the China Grand Prix held at the Shanghai circuit.

He went down after "going over the handlebars" in a chicane of the Chinese track, which caused him a fracture in the left ankle and contusions on the right one.

He had to be treated by doctors in the medical center, but he avoided having to go under the knife and pulled out a great performance to set the fourth fastest time in qualifying and repeat that position at the end of the race.

However, upon returning to his native Spain, he was diagnosed with a fracture of the astragalus bone in his right ankle and a rupture of the lateral ligament in his left ankle.

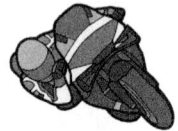

26

**The Assen circuit gave Jorge Lorenzo several
headaches, and the 2013 crash was
one of the biggest.**

He went flying off his Yamaha M1 on a very wet
track at the entry to the fast corners that
dominate the middle part of it.

The impact against the ground of his
left shoulder caused him a fracture
in the collarbone.

Thus, he returned to Barcelona to undergo
surgery, came back to the track the next day,
was cleared by the doctors to race in the
Grand Prix, qualified in twelfth place,
and fought his way up to fifth.

The ovation he received from his box after
the race and the tears of emotion on his
face were well deserved.

27

In the exciting 2006 championship, specifically at the Montmeló race, a multiple crash occurred in the first turn that left everyone stunned.

Sete Gibernau went down after colliding with his Ducati teammate, Loris Capirossi, causing several other riders to suffer the same fate.

The incident led to a red flag and a repeat start, but without several of those affected.

Gibernau, Marco Melandri, and the number 65 were not in a condition to race again.

The first also suffered an additional mishap while being transported to the hospital, as the ambulance he was in collided with a city bus.

The injuries suffered by the Italians harmed their fight for the championship, especially Capi, who had arrived in Barcelona as the leader.

28

The first race after the COVID-19 lockdown, during the 2020 MotoGP Spanish Grand Prix, marked a turning point in Marc Márquez's career.

The Honda rider was leading the race during that Grand Prix held in Jerez behind closed doors, something unheard of in MotoGP, until he ran wide in turn 4 avoiding a crash.

It was lap 5 and there was still a long way to go, but he faced it head-on.

His pace was so incredible that he launched an epic comeback, recovering 13 positions and more than 4 seconds from the front runners, until the crash and continuous problems with his right shoulder.

He suffered a highside just as he was preparing a future pass on Maverick Viñales, and the impact against the asphalt first and then the gravel began his physical ordeal.

29

In 2018, Jorge Lorenzo joined the Ducati team in MotoGP, with the goal of conquering the championship in the top category of world motorcycling.

However, the season did not start well for the Spanish rider.

Lorenzo had difficulty adapting to the Ducati bike and failed to obtain good results in the first races of the championship.

In the new circuit of Thailand, Lorenzo experienced one of the worst crashes of his career.

He lost control of his bike in a turn and somersaulted in the air, and his bike broke in two.

This fall, added to previous ones, ended up undermining Lorenzo's confidence in the Ducati bike and his ability to ride it.

Lorenzo had already crashed a few weeks earlier in Alcañiz after a clash with Márquez in the first lap, which was a severe blow to his championship aspirations.

The fall in Thailand was the last straw for his season at Ducati, as he did not race again for the rest of that year.

After his experience with the Italian team, Lorenzo joined the Honda team in 2019, although he also failed to achieve the expected results and eventually announced his retirement from motorcycling in 2020.

30

**Valentino Rossi crashed in Mugello,
where he had won many times before.**

In the free practice sessions of the 2010 Italian
Grand Prix, il Dottore crashed after being
thrown off his Yamaha.

That afternoon, silence was heard
in the Tuscan circuit.

The number 46 fractured the tibia and fibula of
his right leg, saying goodbye to his chances
of achieving the tenth world championship
crown a year after winning the ninth.

He returned to race and win that season before
bidding farewell to the tuning fork brand,
demonstrating that he was made of a
different kind of material, but it
was never the same again.

31

Rainey vs Schwantz.

Throughout the 80s and early 90s, these two legends battled it out in the premier class of 500cc motorcycling.

However, they knew each other before arriving in the MotoGP world championship.

The two Americans had coincided in their country's AMA Superbike and in the Transatlantic Trophy.

In 1988, both arrived in MotoGP and, during the time they remained, they gave memorable battles, especially the one in Suzuka 1989, as on the Japanese track, they exchanged a lot of overtakes before crossing the finish line.

They took Yamaha and Suzuki to great heights, to the point that Rainey won 3 world championships and Schwantz won 1, although the latter achieved one more victory (25 to 24) than his compatriot and opponent.

The rivalry came to a very unfortunate end: Wayne Rainey suffered a spectacular accident that left him in a wheelchair forever during the 1993 Italian Grand Prix held at the Misano circuit.

The incentive to beat his rival disappeared in Schwantz at once, and he retired two years later, in 1995, after the first three races of the championship.

As often happens, both made peace after finishing their time on the tracks.

32

Rossi vs Biaggi.

Valentino Rossi and Max Biaggi rivaled each other, especially in the early years of Il Dottore among the greatest.

That finger gesture Rossi gave to his opponent in Suzuka 2001 when the Roman pushed him into the grass on the straight before the finish line is now part of history.

They also argued just before getting on the podium of the 2001 Catalan Grand Prix.

As explained to an Italian media, it was because there were more people from Rossi's team than allowed at the prize-giving ceremony.

Nevertheless, they both gave beautiful head-to-head duels for victories, such as in Welkom 2004, which meant the first victory of the one from Tavullia with Yamaha, or Mugello 2005, where both fell on the side of the nine-time champion.

Over time, the bad vibes between them have faded into the background.

In fact, when Rossi announced his retirement, Biaggi dedicated him some beautiful words wishing him the best in his new life and leaving the door open to have a glass of wine together.

33

Crivillé vs Doohan.

Mick Doohan was the great dominator of MotoGP in the 90s, as reflected by his 5 consecutive world titles between 1994 and 1998.

However, he found in his own team, Repsol Honda, and in the Spaniard Alex Crivillé, a tough nut to crack.

Both coexisted for a long time despite their bad relationship, which reached its peak in 1996.

It was when the first Spanish champion of the premier class was in a better position to beat him and, therefore, when the Australian's status was more threatened.

From that season, there are memorable moments, such as the Spanish victory by only 2 thousandths of a second in Brno, Crivillé's fall on the last lap in Jerez when people had entered the track en masse during their duel, or when both collided in Eastern Creek (Australia) and crashed.

The crown of the Catalan finally came in 1999, although in the absence of Doohan, who suffered a serious fall in Jerez that pushed him into retirement.

34

Rossi vs Lorenzo.

After changing Yamaha's life with his titles in 2004 and 2005, Valentino Rossi did not understand why the tuning fork brand was looking for an extremely competitive teammate.

At 21 years old, Jorge Lorenzo entered MotoGP as a two-time world champion of 250cc.

The Spaniard was not willing to play second fiddle to the already thirty-year-old Rossi, and he soon showed it by taking pole position in his debut Grand Prix and winning the race in Estoril.

However, in that first season of 2008, he contained his impulse, but in 2009, he had to sweat to prevent the "99" from touching metal for the first time in the premier class.

In that season, they left an exciting body-to-body duel in Montmeló for posterity, in which they passed and repassed several times until, in the last corner of the last lap, Rossi saw a gap where no one dared to overtake.

However, in 2010, there was no comparison, and with that serious injury during the Mugello training, the battles ended for a few years, although with a brief parenthesis in Motegui, with Lorenzo touching the title with the tips of his fingers.

Seeing that Yamaha was going to bet on Lorenzo, Il Dottore went to Ducati, but he was never among the best when he was dressed in red, so it was not until he returned in 2013 that battles between them were seen again.

35

Lorenzo vs Pedrosa.

There is no doubt that Jorge Lorenzo and Dani Pedrosa were the top representatives of Spanish motorcycle racing before Marc Márquez landed.

In a situation similar to Schwantz and Rainey, the Balearic and the Catalan competed long before reaching MotoGP, and they battled for victories in both 125 and 250cc categories.

If there was a moment of special tension between them, it was during the only season they both competed in the 250cc category, when Pedrosa won his second title in the category and the third of his career.

Lorenzo was left with the bitter taste of defeat several times and could not win any race in 2005, but he did not hesitate to declare that he was better than Pedrosa.

Lorenzo had to wait a few years to prove that his words were not far from reality, as he beat Pedrosa twice when they were competing for the MotoGP title: in 2010 and 2012.

In the latter, the diminutive Honda rider came closer than ever to winning, but a crash in Misano ruined his chances, which he had earned with a great victory in Brno against Lorenzo with an incredible overtaking move on the last corner.

36

Rossi vs Stoner.

Casey Stoner became one of the best MotoGP riders with Ducati, as he dominated with the Italian brand in 2007 and gave them their first and only title so far.

This was a situation that clashed with Rossi, who had dominated the championship in recent times, with the exception of 2006.

For Il Dottore, it was a reality check that made him focus more and more on physical preparation, as he acknowledged in the docu-series dedicated to him for his retirement.

And that's what he did to regain his throne in 2008, as well as the psychological game that had given him so much advantage over his opponents throughout his career.

If there is one duel especially remembered between them, it was at Laguna Seca, with that incredible overtake by the Italian at the Corkscrew corner, which, as the Australian admitted, made him "lose respect" for the nine-time champion.

In 2011, with Stoner already on Honda, another moment of tension arose between them, as during the Jerez race, Rossi caused Stoner to crash.

The track was difficult due to the rain, but Il Dottore dared to overtake.

When he went to Stoner's box to apologize, he famously said, "your ambition is greater than your talent."

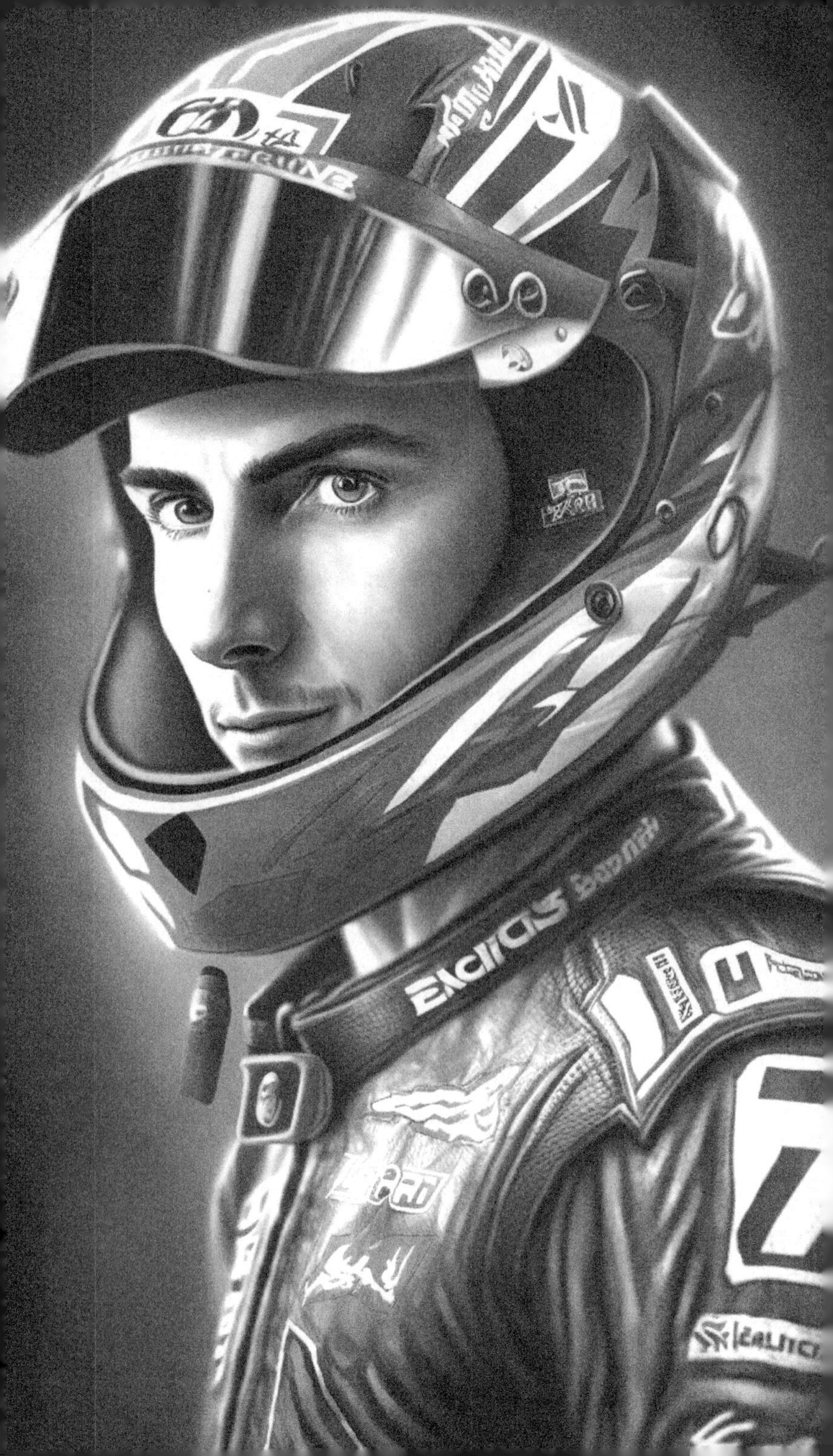

37

Márquez vs Rossi.

Although they never played for a championship until the end, the duels between Marc Márquez and Valentino Rossi made history, especially in 2015 in the races in Argentina, the Netherlands, and Malaysia.

At Termas de Río Hondo, it was already clear that something was happening between them with that touch that ended up with Cervera on the ground and exploded in Sepang with that kick that, with a penalty, prevented the Italian from winning his tenth title.

Young Márquez admired Rossi, but when such important things are at stake, admirations are put aside as was demonstrated.

In 2018, it was Márquez who threw Rossi in Argentina and was also sanctioned for it, but the reaction of the Yamaha box when he went to apologize was hostile.

They never made peace and it seems that it will continue to be so.

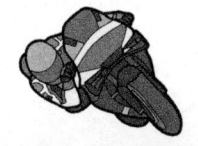

38

The most modest amounts that pilots earn start from €200,000, which correspond to those who drive for teams that rarely appear in the top positions in races, as well as rookies.

In this group, you can perfectly find people like Esponsorama Racing rider Luca Marini, who made his debut when Rossi's younger brother scored a total of 41 points, with a 5th place as his best result.

In that mentioned salary range, there are also the 3 rookies in the category.

They are, on the one hand, the teammates in the Tech 3 KTM satellite team Remy Gardner and Raúl Fernández, and on the other hand, Darryn Binder, who raced for Yamaha's homologous structure, the WITHU Yamaha RNF, after moving up directly from Moto3.

It should be noted that among the four KTM competitors, including the official ones (Miguel Ángel Oliveira and Brad Binder) and themselves, they do not even add up to €3.6 million.

At Aprilia, they go up to €4,000,000 split between Maverick Viñales and Aleix Espargaró.

There are very striking cases, such as that of the 2020 runner-up, Franco Morbidelli, who, racing for the official Yamaha team, received just under 1.5 million euros, which is also a product of the strategy that each manufacturer has decided to adopt to deal with the economic crisis.

At Honda, they have decided to distribute just over three million to satisfy the salaries of Pol Espargaró, Álex Márquez, and Takaaki Nakagami.

The bulk goes to the Repsol team member, as will be seen later, while both LCR competitors do not even reach one million euros.

39

Pol Espargaró is a Spanish motorcycle racer, currently competing for the Honda team in MotoGP.

Pol's signing by the official Honda team in 2021 was one of the highlights of the season, and it is rumored that his contract guaranteed him a salary of 2.5 million euros per season.

Despite being an experienced and successful rider, Pol Espargaró's adaptation to the Honda team was not easy, as the bike is considered one of the most difficult to ride on the grid.

However, throughout the season, Pol showed good performance and achieved his first pole position at the Catalunya Grand Prix, as well as a podium at the Styrian Grand Prix.

In the 2022 season, Pol tried to improve his results from the previous season, but unfortunately suffered a serious crash during the Valencia Grand Prix practice in Cheste.

As a result of the crash, he suffered injuries that prevented him from competing in the last races of the season.

Despite the injury, Pol Espargaró has established himself as one of the standout riders on the MotoGP grid and is expected to continue fighting for the top positions in the coming seasons.

40

Enea Bastianini's signing by Ducati involved a payment of 3.8 million euros, demonstrating the confidence that the Italian factory has in the young Italian rider.

Bastianini, Moto2 champion in 2020, made his debut in the MotoGP category last season with the Esponsorama Racing team, where he demonstrated his talent and ability to quickly adapt to the new bike and the most demanding category in world motorcycle racing.

In his first MotoGP season, he achieved 2 top 10 finishes and finished in 14th position in the overall classification.

For the 2022 season, Bastianini joined the official Ducati team, alongside experienced Italian rider Francesco Bagnaia.

Although his adaptation to the Desmosedici GP21 was not easy at first, he managed to achieve good results in practice and demonstrated his potential by qualifying in third position at the San Marino Grand Prix, behind Yamaha riders Fabio Quartararo and Maverick Viñales.

It is true that Ducati's strategy focused on developing their bike rather than making big signings, demonstrating the Italian factory's confidence in the talent of their riders and their ability to improve the bike.

This, combined with Bastianini's great performance, shows that the young rider has a bright future in the premier class of world motorcycle racing.

41

Jorge Martin is a Spanish MotoGP rider born in Madrid in 1998.

After standing out in the lower categories of motorcycle racing, he made his debut in the premier class in the 2021 season with the Pramac Racing team, which uses Ducati motorcycles.

Despite it being his first season in MotoGP, Martin achieved excellent results, including his first victory in the category at the Austrian Grand Prix, where he led the race from the start and showed himself to be far superior to his rivals.

He also achieved several poles and podiums, which allowed him to stand out as the best rookie of the year.

However, at the Portuguese Grand Prix, during free practice, he suffered a spectacular crash that caused a wrist fracture and forced him to miss several races.

Despite this, his performance throughout the season and his great talent on the bike earned him a contract for the 2022 season with the official Ducati team.

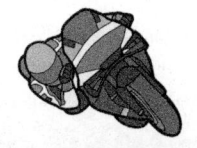

42

Johann Zarco is a 31-year-old French rider who made his MotoGP debut in 2017 with the Monster Yamaha Tech 3 team.

Before reaching the premier class, he won two Moto2 titles in 2015 and 2016.

In his first MotoGP season, Zarco impressed by achieving two podiums and six top-5 finishes, ending up in the top-10 of the general classification in his debut.

In 2018, Zarco continued with Tech 3, but with an older specification Yamaha.

Despite the difficulties, he achieved a total of seven top-5 finishes, although he couldn't get on the podium.

After that season, he decided to change teams and signed with the official KTM team.

However, his time at KTM was not as successful as expected, and he decided to return to Yamaha in 2020, this time with the Avintia Racing team.

In his new team, Zarco had an irregular season, although he achieved a podium in Brno and two pole positions.

In 2021, Zarco signed with the Ducati Pramac Racing team and started the season impressively, leading the championship after the first races and achieving two podiums.

Although his performance decreased in the second half of the season, he managed to stay among the top 10 in the general classification.

Regarding his salary, it is estimated that in 2021 Johann Zarco earned 3.8 million euros, a figure that puts him on the same level as other outstanding riders such as Enea Bastianini or Jorge Martin.

43

Jack Miller is a motorcycle racer born in Townsville, Australia on January 18, 1995.

In 2011, he participated in the Australian Supersport Championship and in 2012 he made his debut in the Moto3 World Championship.

With the Caretta Technology team, he achieved his first victory in the United States Grand Prix in 2013.

In 2015, Miller made the jump to MotoGP with the LCR Honda team.

In his first season, he achieved a podium at the Dutch Grand Prix and finished in eighteenth place in the championship.

In 2016, he signed with the Marc VDS Racing team, where he achieved his first pole position in the Argentina Grand Prix and his first victory in the Dutch Grand Prix.

In 2018, Jack Miller joined the Alma Pramac Racing team, where he began competing with the Ducati Desmosedici GP17 bike.

In 2020, he achieved two podiums and finished in eighth place in the championship.

In 2021, he renewed with the team and achieved two victories and three more podiums, which allowed him to finish fourth in the final championship standings.

Miller is known for his aggressive style and extroverted personality off the track.

He is also one of the most popular riders among Australian fans, thanks to his talent and charisma.

44

Francesco "Pecco" Bagnaia is an Italian MotoGP rider who currently races for the official Ducati team.

In the 2021 season, he achieved four victories, two poles, and five podiums, which led him to win his first world title in the premier class of motorcycle racing.

Bagnaia is considered one of the most talented riders of his generation and has had a great progression in his career since his debut in Moto3 in 2013.

In his sporting career, Bagnaia has passed through different teams and categories.

In 2017, he made his debut in Moto2 with the Sky Racing VR46 team, owned by Valentino Rossi, and in 2018 he achieved his first victory in the category at the Qatar Grand Prix.

In 2019, with the Ducati Pramac Racing team, he achieved two victories and six podiums, which led him to finish second in the Moto2 championship.

In 2020, Bagnaia made the jump to the premier class with the Pramac Racing team, where he achieved a podium and showed great potential.

In the 2021 season, already with the official Ducati team, he took a leap in quality and consolidated himself as one of the main protagonists of the season.

With his consecutive victories in Aragon, Misano, Portimao, and Cheste, he became the first Italian rider to win four consecutive races in the premier class since Valentino Rossi did it in 2008.

However, in the second race held at the Marco Simoncelli circuit, Bagnaia was leading the race when he fell and gave the title to Fabio Quartararo, who won the race.

Despite this setback, Bagnaia finished the season in second place in the championship, with 310 points, 45 points behind Quartararo.

45

Álex Rins.

He is a Spanish rider who currently races for the Suzuki team in MotoGP.

He joined the premier class in 2017 and has since demonstrated his talent on several occasions.

Rins has achieved a total of 5 victories in his MotoGP career, the most recent being at the 2021 British Grand Prix in Silverstone.

Additionally, he has stood on the podium on numerous occasions and has achieved several pole positions.

The Suzuki team is known for trying to balance their bike and finances between their riders, so although Rins is not at the top of the list of highest-paid riders, his success on the track brings him closer to that podium.

Additionally, Rins has had to overcome some injuries in his career, such as the fracture of his right arm radius in the 2020 Spanish Grand Prix.

Regarding the victories mentioned in the question, the victory in Austin 2019 was very memorable due to the great battle Rins had with Valentino Rossi throughout the race, overtaking the Italian in the last corner to achieve his first victory in the premier class.

The victory in Silverstone 2019 was also very exciting, as Rins fought in a spectacular duel with the then-champion Marc Marquez, whom he managed to overtake in the last lap to achieve the victory.

46

Fabrizio Borra.

He is an Italian motorcycle engineer and coach.

He is known in the MotoGP world for having worked as a personal coach for several riders, including Valentino Rossi, Jorge Lorenzo, and Andrea Iannone.

Borra began his career in the world of motorcycle racing in 1995 as a suspension engineer on the Aprilia team.

He then moved to the Yamaha racing team, where he worked as the chief suspension engineer for several years.

In 2010, he began working with Valentino Rossi as a personal coach and has been working with him ever since.

Borra has also worked with other riders, such as Jorge Lorenzo and Andrea Iannone.

It is said that Borra has a great ability to identify the strengths and weaknesses of riders and help them improve their riding.

Additionally, he has developed a specific training methodology for motorcycling that is based on specific exercises to improve strength, flexibility, endurance, and concentration.

47

Fabio Quartararo is a French motorcycle racer who currently competes in the MotoGP category for the Yamaha Factory Racing team.

In the 2021 season, Quartararo dominated the championship with authority, achieving 11 poles, 8 victories, and 15 podiums in 18 races.

This allowed him to win the MotoGP world championship with a lead of 101 points over the second-placed rider, Joan Mir.

Quartararo began his MotoGP career in 2019 with the Petronas Yamaha SRT team, with which he achieved his first victory in the Catalunya Grand Prix in that same season.

In 2020, also with the Petronas Yamaha SRT team, he achieved 3 victories and 5 podiums in total, finishing in fifth position in the championship.

For the 2021 season, Quartararo was signed by the official Yamaha Factory Racing team, where he shared the team with Italian rider Franco Morbidelli.

Despite having some ups and downs during the season, Quartararo managed to dominate most of the races and became the first French rider to win the MotoGP championship since the legendary French rider Jacques Villeneuve in 1997.

48

Joan Mir is a Spanish motorcycle racer born on September 1, 1997, in Palma de Mallorca.

He began his career in motorcycles in 2015, in the Moto3 category of the Motorcycle World Championship.

That same year, he achieved his first victory in the Czech Republic Grand Prix and finished in seventh position in the final championship standings.

In 2018, he made the jump to the Moto2 category, where he achieved two victories and finished in sixth position in the final standings.

The following year, in 2019, he joined the Suzuki MotoGP team, where he demonstrated his great talent and skill by achieving his first victory in the category in the Australian Grand Prix and finishing in fifth position in the final championship standings.

In the 2020 season, Joan Mir was crowned MotoGP world champion, becoming the third Spanish rider to achieve this feat after Álex Crivillé and Jorge Lorenzo.

He achieved his first victory in the category in the European Grand Prix and accumulated a total of 7 podiums throughout the season.

In addition, he was the most consistent rider, managing to finish all the races of the championship among the top 7.

Due to his great performance in the 2020 season, Joan Mir received a significant salary increase for the 2021 season, earning 6.5 million euros and becoming one of the highest-paid riders in the category.

His ability to get the most out of the Suzuki and his consistency in the races have established him as one of the greats of the category and a rider to watch in the coming seasons.

49

Marc Márquez is a Spanish MotoGP rider, born in Cervera on February 17, 1993.

He is one of the most successful riders in the history of the premier class, with 8 world titles, all of them achieved with Honda.

In 2020, Márquez was injured in the first race of the season and had to miss the rest of the championship, which led him to ask Honda not to receive his salary due to his inactivity.

However, Honda rejected the proposal and Márquez continued to receive his salary.

In 2021, Márquez returned to competition after more than a year of absence due to his injury.

He won three races in the season and achieved one more podium at the Alcañiz circuit, where he had an exciting duel with Francesco Bagnaia.

Márquez has been a prominent figure in MotoGP for many years due to his ability to ride the bike in difficult conditions and his capacity to achieve impressive victories.

50

Valentino Rossi - 372 races.

Not only is he the best of the modern era of motorcycle racing, but also the one who has competed in the most races in the premier class.

Valentino Rossi stopped the counter at 372 after competing in the 2021 Valencia Grand Prix on the Cheste circuit.

In addition, he is the only one on this list who can boast of having won the championship titles with both names.

He was the last to be crowned the best in the 500cc category back in 2001 with Honda, and subsequently, he was the great dominator of the first 4 editions of MotoGP.

The golden wing brand and Yamaha are the brands with which he became a legend from 2001 to 2003, as well as in two stages from 2004 to 2005 and from 2008 to 2009.

He also wore red with Ducati in 2011 and 2012, although without being able to win.

51

Andrea Dovizioso – 248 races.

Andrea Dovizioso hung up his helmet after the 2022 San Marino Grand Prix held in Misano.

Dovi decided to retire before the end of the season as he couldn't get more out of the satellite Yamaha he was riding.

However, he will always remember becoming the second rider with the most races contested in the premier class of motorcycle racing, which he entered in 2008 with Honda.

He made his debut with Honda's satellite team before moving up to the factory team in 2009, where he achieved his first win on a rainy summer Sunday at Donington Park.

He stayed with the Japanese team until the end of 2011, before joining Yamaha's satellite team.

His stay there was brief, and in 2013 he signed with Ducati, where he showed all his potential by achieving 14 more victories and three consecutive runner-up finishes (2017-2019).

After a discreet 2020, he didn't renew with Ducati and decided to take a sabbatical year until he was offered the opportunity to race with the WithU Yamaha RNF MotoGP Team, which he signed for in late 2021.

52

Álex Barros – 246 races.

Although he was never a champion nor close to being one, Brazilian rider Álex Barros stayed for a long time, with ups and downs, in the premier class of motorcycle racing.

He debuted in the category in 1990, and the last season he participated in was 2007.

After that, he left a record with 246 races contested behind him.

He debuted with Cagiva, for which he raced for three seasons (1990, 1991, and 1992).

In 1993 he signed with Suzuki, where he stayed for a couple of years (1993 and 1994) and achieved his first victory at Jarama before signing with Honda (1995), specifically their satellite team at that time.

He stayed with the Japanese team for many years, until 2002, with the satellite structure of each season (Kanemoto, Pileri, and Pons).

He won five times before leaving for Yamaha, where he only raced for one year (2003).

He returned in 2004 to race with the factory team and in 2005 returned to Sito Pons' team structure.

Ducati and their satellite team Pramac were his last companions on his journey (2007).

53

Nicky Hayden and Dani Pedrosa - 218 races.

In fourth place we have a tie between two riders who shared a team: Nicky Hayden and Dani Pedrosa.

Unfortunately, the former is no longer with us since that fateful accident in Italy in 2017, but he left great moments in MotoGP history throughout his journey between 2003 and 2016, such as his 2006 title with Honda at the Cheste circuit against Valentino Rossi.

He achieved 3 victories: Laguna Seca in 2005 and 2006 as well as Assen in the championship-winning season.

His style with slides in the corners delighted motorcycle enthusiasts.

There are also many wonders that can be told about Pedrosa, despite the fact that the championship title eluded him.

With the official Honda team, he ran the vast majority of his MotoGP career, which led him to the runner-up positions in 2007, 2010, and 2012.

Injuries weighed down a naturally talented rider who achieved 31 wins, climbed the podium 112 times, and had 31 poles.

He retired in 2018, although he later signed with KTM as a tester and ran the 2021 Styrian GP, which was his return to the World Championship.

54

Loris Capirossi - 217 races.

Another rider who never became a champion but had a consistent trajectory in the premier category was Loris Capirossi.

The Italian reached 500 cubic centimeters in 1995 with the label of an emerging promise after his 125cc titles, the first as the youngest in history at 17 years and 5 months, and his 2 great campaigns in 250cc, as he was runner-up (1993) and third (1994).

Honda, with its satellite team, gave him the opportunity to debut, and he certainly took advantage of it as he achieved his first podium and finished sixth in the final standings.

He then moved to Yamaha, where he couldn't replicate his performance, so he dropped to 250cc, where he won the title.

He returned to the premier class with Honda, in Sito Pons' team, who led him to his first victory, before participating in Ducati's early steps in MotoGP, to which he gave its first 6 wins.

After that, he signed with Suzuki (2008-2010) before bidding farewell with Ducati at Pramac.

55

Aleix Espargaró – 214 races.

The veteran Aprilia rider tied with Capirossi at Valencia in 2022 and surpassed him in the opening race of 2023.

The rider from Granollers began his trajectory in the premier class in 2009, specifically during the 2009 Indianapolis Grand Prix riding a Pramac Ducati.

His consistency earned him a contract for 2010, but his results did not improve and he dropped down to Moto2 in 2011.

He returned to stay in MotoGP and rode one of the CRT (Claiming Rule Teams) in 2012 and 2013 with the Jorge Martínez Aspar team before trying his luck in one of Yamaha's satellite teams and then Suzuki.

He carried Aprilia on his back since joining in 2017, leading the team to their first podium in the premier class at Silverstone 2021 and their first victory in Termas del Río Hondo 2022.

56

Jorge Lorenzo - 203 races.

The number 99 stopped counting at 203 races after retiring in Cheste 2019 at the age of 32.

Had he not retired at such a relatively early age and the crashes that pushed him to it, he would surely have a higher place in this ranking.

In 2008 he debuted in MotoGP with the official Yamaha alongside Valentino Rossi, and it was in 2010 when he first won the championship with the tuning forks factory.

His resounding success was followed by the titles of 2012 and 2015.

In 2017, he joined Ducati, with whom he won three races in 2018 before trying his luck with Honda, his last team.

57

Colin Edwards - 196 races.

Like his compatriot Nicky Hayden, Colin Edwards came to MotoGP from Superbikes, where he won two titles.

In 2004 he shared a team with Sete Gibernau in the Gresini Honda satellite team and between 2005 and 2007 with Valentino Rossi in the official Yamaha structure.

Later, he raced with Kawasaki and in Yamaha's satellite squad.

After the 2014 season, he stopped his count at 196 races.

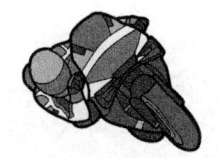

58

Carlos Checa wore the number 7 on his fairing throughout 194 races between 1995 and 2010, both in 500cc and MotoGP.

He debuted with Honda and won his two victories at Jarama (1998) and Montmeló (1996), although he raced for Yamaha longer (1999-2004 and 2006).

He also went through Ducati, specifically in 2005 and 2010, first with the factory team and then with Pramac replacing Mika Kallio at Estoril and Cheste.

He had more success in the Superbike World Championship, which he won in 2011, but nobody takes away the honor of appearing on this list.

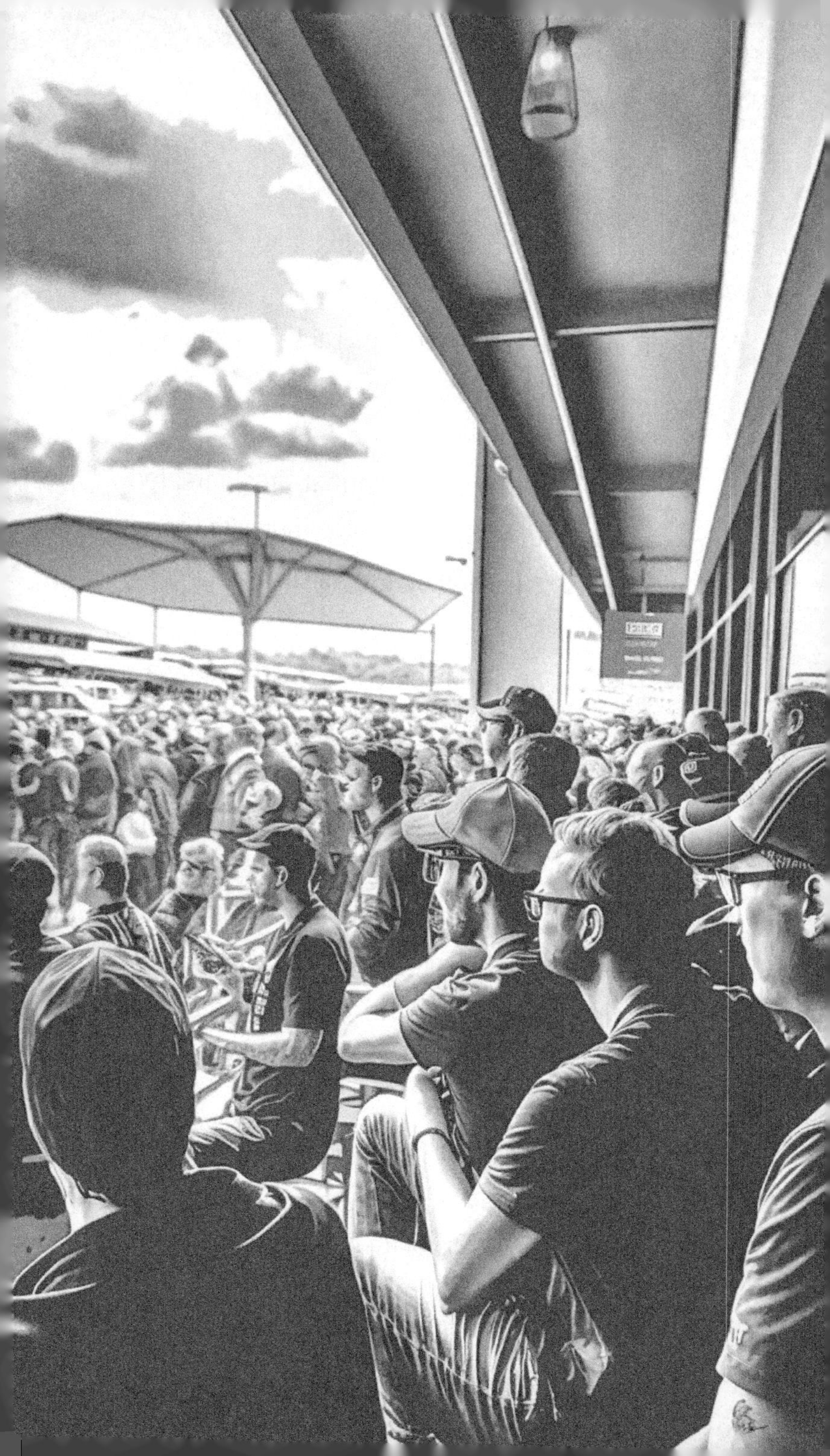

59

Estoril 2006.

It was the only victory of Toni Elías among the greats on two wheels.

The Honda Gresini rider at that time defeated Valentino Rossi by just two thousandths of a second on the finish line.

That movie-like ending was preceded by a beautiful battle between the Spaniard and il dottore, who were accompanied for much of the race by Kenny Roberts Jr. and his Suzuki.

Earlier, the other title contender, and eventual champion in the last race in Valencia, Nicky Hayden, had crashed after being taken down by his teammate at Honda, Dani Pedrosa.

Those 5 points that Rossi did not earn by less than a breath were decisive and, perhaps, would have allowed the Tavullia rider to boast of 10 crowns.

60

If there's something that makes motorcycling special, it's the greater ease of seeing overtaking maneuvers.

That's why Assen in 2018 saw Marc Marquez win after an intense group battle that was the scene of 157 overtakes, including fairings rubbing together.

The show was also put on by Maverick Viñales, Rossi, Andrea Dovizioso, Jack Miller, Pol Espargaro, and Alex Rins.

However, the Cervera rider managed to distance himself from the rest of the pursuers, to the point of achieving a final distance of 13 seconds, imposing an unreachable pace for his rivals.

It was the prelude to what was going to happen at the end of that year, with Marquez proclaiming himself world champion for the seventh time and fifth occasion in the premier class.

He was accompanied on the podium by Rins and Viñales, respectively, which meant a full Spanish podium sweep.

61

Phillip Island 2015.

The year 2015 was historic for many reasons, some more pleasant than others.

The antepenultimate race of that season marked much of what happened afterwards.

Like the previous one, there were many overtakes and unexpected guests in the fight for victory.

Jorge Lorenzo, Rossi, Andrea Iannone, and Marquez overtook each other on 52 occasions.

As an anecdote, a seagull collided with Iannone's Ducati when he was leading the race.

What happened angered Rossi, who was playing for the title against Lorenzo, to the point of accusing Honda's rider of deliberately favoring the interests of the Mallorcan.

What happened in the Sepang race between both riders the following week was the last straw.

62

The Montmeló 2009 race was the seventh round of that season's MotoGP World Championship.

The race took place at the Barcelona-Catalonia circuit and was famous for the intense battle between Yamaha teammates Valentino Rossi and Jorge Lorenzo.

For most of the race, Lorenzo led and seemed on track to win.

However, Rossi didn't give up and continued fighting until the last lap, when he managed to overtake Lorenzo on the final corner to take the victory by just 0.095 seconds.

Casey Stoner completed the podium in third place.

Rossi's victory in this race was particularly significant because it brought him to lead the championship for the first time that season.

The rivalry between Rossi and Lorenzo was at its peak at that time, as both were extremely talented riders and competed in the same team, increasing the tension between them.

63

Losail 2019.

Andrea Dovizioso has proven to be a great competitor in MotoGP when he rode for Ducati, obtaining runner-up finishes in 2017, 2018, and 2019.

In the last of those, he fell farther behind Márquez, but in the opening race held at the Losail Circuit, he prevailed over the Spaniard in the last corner.

They were accompanied in the hunt by the British rider Cal Crutchlow, who finished third, Rins, and Rossi.

The red bike's straight-line power imposed its law, as it has generally been doing on the Qatari layout in recent years.

The battles between the two have been repeated many times over the years, demonstrating that on the track, perhaps there isn't as much distance as the points have shown at the end of several titles that have fallen on the side of the Honda rider.

64

Laguna Seca 2008.

Casey Stoner and Ducati were a powerful duo in the MotoGP world, crowned in 2007 with surprising authority over their rivals.

However, the end of their reign came in the 2008 Laguna Seca race.

Rossi made that legendary overtake on the Australian at the Corkscrew, which may also be the riskiest in history considering the slope of that part of the American circuit.

That moment was crucial in the course of the championship, with Rossi returning to reign after 2 years without doing so.

However, a few laps later, the Australian crashed, and the victory was handed to the Italian on a platter, who crossed the finish line with a lead of 13 seconds over him and 26 over his compatriot Chris Vermeulen of Suzuki.

65

Catalonia 2007.

Here, Stoner celebrated victory over Rossi, but not without suffering, as everything was up in the air until he crossed the finish line.

The proof is that he won by only 69 thousandths of a second.

The script of the race was similar to what had been seen in Losail many times: absolute superiority of Ducati on the straights and a dogfight in the corners of the circuit.

Pedrosa was also on their tail, who also had real chances of winning as he passed within three tenths of Stoner.

The three protagonists showed that day why they were the best in the world.

66

Considered by many as the king without a crown, Dani Pedrosa holds several admirable records.

He is the only rider who has achieved at least one victory over 16 seasons in the world championship.

He is the third rider with the most podiums in the premier class with 112, only surpassed by Lorenzo (114) and Rossi (149).

The most epic victory of the diminutive rider was undoubtedly Brno 2012, a year that also saw his best performance and that, perhaps, should have earned him that coveted MotoGP crown that injuries and luck deprived him of.

On the Czech track, he fought against his compatriot and rival Jorge Lorenzo in a battle that made fans go wild.

The win was not decided until the last corner, with an impressive outside overtake by number 26 taking advantage of his rival's wider line and slower exit speed.

67

The pandemic has not prevented enjoying thrilling races.

The first season held during it had many alternatives, with unsuspected title contenders like Joan Mir.

A variety that was appreciated, although with the terrible news of Márquez's injury in the opening round in Jerez.

At the Alcañiz circuit, two contenders with a not so extensive record of victories, rookie Álex Márquez and Suzuki's namesake Rins, were seen.

The balance tilted in favor of the latter after many overtakes between them, which served to see what the younger Márquez is capable of among the best.

As if there wasn't enough epic, Rins had to come back from the tenth position on the starting grid to win.

True to his consistency, Mir accompanied them on the podium.

68

In the Jerez 2010 race, Jorge Lorenzo was seen winning and, in turn, embarking on the path to his first MotoGP championship.

Both the development and the subsequent celebration were epic: the former because he came from behind, getting rid of Hayden and Rossi before doing the same with a dominant Pedrosa, and the latter because he jumped into the lake at the Andalusian track with his suit on.

The latter posed difficulties for him to get out of there since he needed help to do it.

Apart from that, it was the emotional boost that the five-time champion needed to achieve the ultimate feat that he confirmed in Sepang.

What happened that Sunday in May was, like other races that have appeared here, a gift that an irreplaceable cast of champions offered: Rossi, Stoner, Pedrosa, and Lorenzo himself.

69

The history of MotoGP dates back to 1949 when the International Motorcycling Federation (FIM) organized the first World Championship.

Since then, each edition has had different categories defined according to the engine's displacement.

In these more than 70 years of history, there was everything, even categories with displacements as low as 50cc.

Before its current denomination, the category had a more descriptive (and much less attractive) name: It was called 500cc.

In 2002, the displacement was increased to 990cc.

It was the perfect excuse to look for a sexier name.

The FIM opted for MotoGP, the name by which the premier class has been known since then.

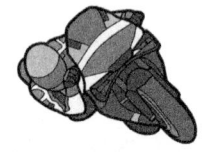

70

The Misano Marco Simoncelli Circuit is a race track located in the Emilia-Romagna region of Italy.

It was inaugurated in 1972 and has since undergone several renovations, including a major overhaul in 2006.

The circuit has a length of 4.2 kilometers and features 16 turns, 6 left and 10 right.

It is characterized by a mix of fast and slow corners, as well as two long straights, making it a demanding track for riders and bikes.

As for records, as mentioned in the statement, Jorge Lorenzo holds the circuit's fastest lap record with a time of 1:31.868, set during qualifying for the San Marino Grand Prix in 2016.

As for the race, Italian rider Andrea Dovizioso holds the record with a time of 1:32.678, set in the San Marino Grand Prix in 2018.

Misano is one of the circuits that is part of the MotoGP World Championship calendar and has hosted races in the premier class since 2007.

In addition, races from other categories such as the Superbike World Championship are also held there.

71

The Termas de Rio Hondo International Circuit.

Located in Argentina, construction began in 2007 and was completed in May 2008.

It has a length of 4.806 meters, with nine right-hand turns and five left-hand turns.

It is one of the longest straight circuits in the world, exceeding 1.076 meters.

With a track width of 16 meters, of those 14 turns, there are 4 that play a fundamental role in each race and fuel the spectacle: the odd numbered 1, 5, 7, and 13.

Turns 5 and 7 are hot spots for riders: very tight and right-hand corners where technique and brakes are key.

It was there, in turn 7, where Marc Marquez and Valentino Rossi had their unforgettable battle in 2015 after the Italian's comeback and the Spanish rider's subsequent fall in the epic victory of the great idol.

72

Why is it called MotoGP?

The name comes from the abbreviation of Grand Prix Motorcycle Racing.

This championship is the top category of the sport and brings together the world's 22 best riders, divided into 11 teams.

The Motorcycle World Championship is held every year between March and November.

There are three categories: MotoGP, which is the top class, as well as Moto2 and Moto3, which are the entry-level categories where younger riders take their first steps in the championship.

73

Each Grand Prix is held over 3 days and has 3 main parts: Free practice sessions, qualifying sessions, and finally, the races.

The MotoGP race lasts around 45 minutes and covers around 115 km.

The riders line up in rows of three on the grid, according to the position they have achieved in the qualifying sessions.

The MotoGP classification is based on a points system.

At the end of the season, the winner will be the rider who has accumulated the most points in the classification.

During the race, practice or qualifying, the failure to comply with the rules is punished with penalties that can affect the rider's classification.

74

Motegi Circuit.

In 1999, two years after its construction, the first Japanese GP was held at the Motegi circuit, but between 2000 and 2003 the Land of the Rising Sun had two Grand Prix on its soil, one in April at Suzuka, which took the name of the Japanese GP, and another in October in Motegi which became known as the Pacific GP.

The sad death of Daijiro Katoh in the Suzuka race in 2003 meant the end of World Championship races at this circuit and Motegi became the exclusive host of the Japanese GP from 2004 onwards.

It has 6 long accelerations, followed by 6 sharp braking sections.

It is the circuit where 1st gear is used the most, up to 3 times, and where the most gear changes are made, a total of 30 per lap.

The circuit that is most similar to it is Le Mans.

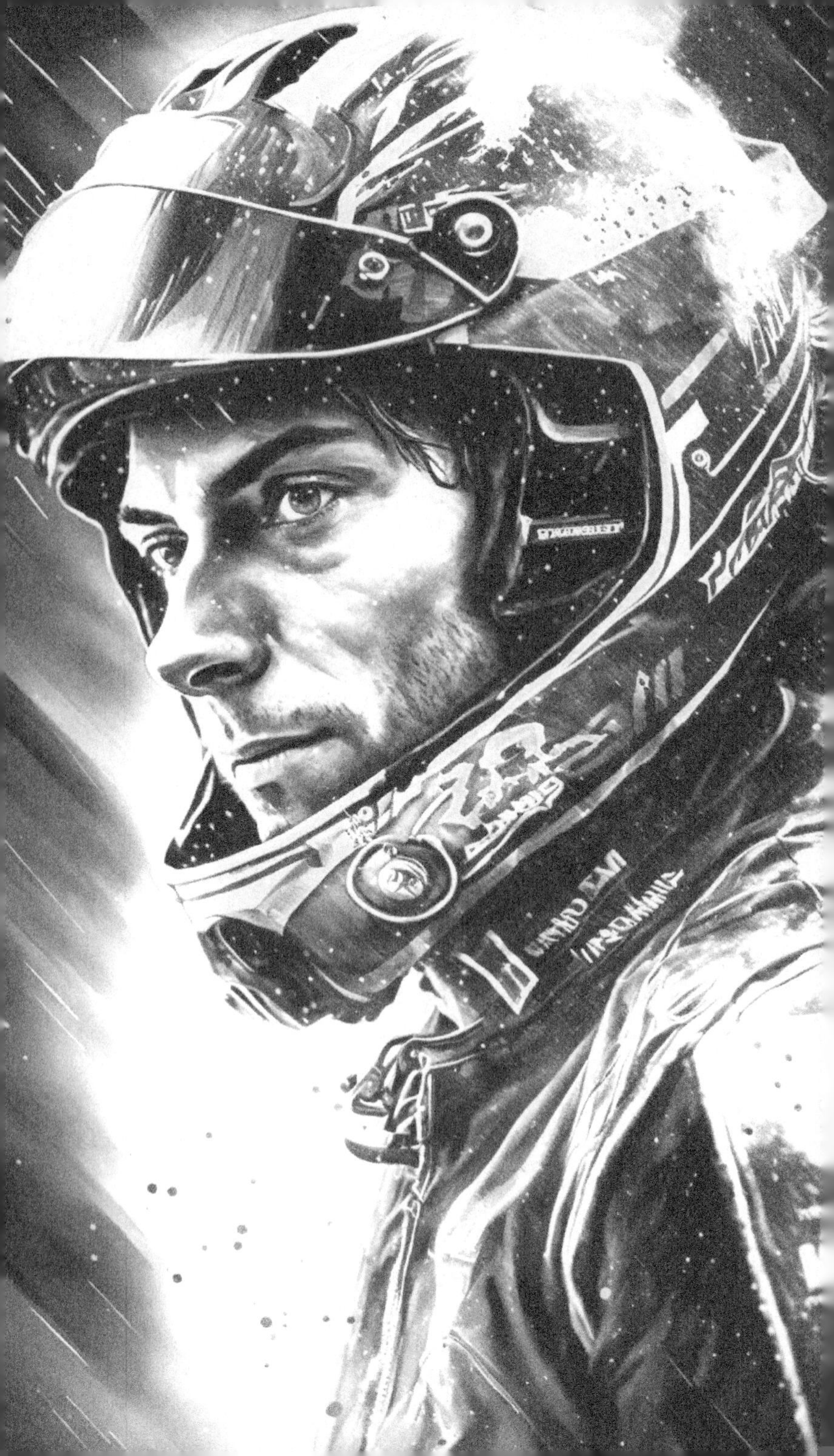

75

Can anyone become a MotoGP rider?

Becoming a MotoGP rider is not something that can be improvised, and the apparent ease with which they ride on the circuits is the result of years of hard work.

While some qualities are innate, such as talent, others, especially physical ones, are gained through intensive training.

To master a bike that weighs 157 kg, has 270 horsepower, and reaches speeds of 350 km/h, you have to be in perfect physical shape.

All MotoGP riders are elite athletes, although their training varies from one to another.

While Aleix Espargaró does a lot of road cycling, Frenchman Johann Zarco prefers climbing.

76

The Motorcycle World Championship has gone through several categories throughout its history.

The oldest category is the 500cc, which was contested from the creation of the championship in 1949 until 2001.

From that year on, the displacement was reduced to 990cc and in 2007 it was reduced again to 800cc until the current MotoGP category was adopted in 2012, with 1000cc engines.

The 250cc category was introduced in 1949 and was contested until 2011, when it was replaced by the current Moto2, which uses 600cc engines.

The 125cc category was introduced in 1949 and was contested until 2011, when it was replaced by the current Moto3, which uses 250cc engines.

In addition, there were lesser-known categories such as the 50cc, which was contested between 1962 and 1983, and the 80cc, which was contested between 1984 and 1989.

There was also a 350cc category that was contested from the creation of the championship in 1949 until 1982.

The 750cc category was introduced in 1973, but did not score points for the overall classification of the world championship, but rather was contested in special races.

This category was maintained until 1979, when it was replaced by the 1000cc category.

77

What has been the highest number of participants in history?

It was in the 1969 Tourist Trophy on the Isle of Man, with 97 riders in the 500cc category.

However, it's important to note that the number of participants can vary depending on the race and category.

For example, currently, the maximum number of riders allowed on the MotoGP grid is 22, while in Moto2 and Moto3 it's 32.

It's also common for races to have fewer participants due to factors such as injuries or team budgets.

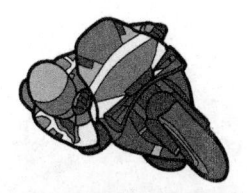

78

Track officials are a fundamental part of safety in motorcycle racing, and their work is very important.

In addition to being volunteers, they have to go through a selection and training process before they can work in a race.

In the case of MotoGP, track officials are responsible for different tasks, such as signaling flags, indicating the starting grid position, supervising the pit entry and exit, and assisting in case of accidents or emergency situations.

These officials are a key piece in the safety of the riders and spectators, and their work is crucial for races to take place safely and orderly.

In addition, their work is performed voluntarily, which demonstrates the passion they feel for the sport of motorcycle racing.

79

The Circuit de Catalunya, also known as the Barcelona-Catalunya Circuit, is a racing circuit located in Montmelo, Spain, about 30 kilometers north of Barcelona.

The circuit was inaugurated in 1991 and has since hosted numerous car and motorcycle racing events, including the MotoGP Spanish Grand Prix.

In the 1999 season, Alex Criville became the first Spanish rider to win the MotoGP world championship in the premier class.

During that same year, Criville also won the race at the Circuit de Catalunya, in an exciting race that was decided by 61 thousandths of a second, beating his teammate Tadayuki Okada.

With this victory, Criville became the first Spanish rider to win a MotoGP race in his home country.

The 1999 race in Montmelo was also memorable for the Repsol Honda team's impressive sweep, with Criville, Okada, and Sete Gibernau taking the top three spots on the podium.

The race was also highlighted by the intense battle between Criville and Okada on the last lap, where the Spanish rider managed to overtake his teammate in the final turn to take the victory.

80

In 2013, Marc Marquez made history by winning the MotoGP race at Laguna Seca circuit, becoming the first rookie to achieve this feat.

This was also the last time a Grand Prix was held at this circuit, as it has been off the world championship calendar since 2014.

The race at Laguna Seca is one of the most iconic events on the MotoGP calendar, with the famous Corkscrew turn that defies gravity and has been the scene of great battles and exciting moments over the years.

Marquez, who debuted in the premier class that same year, demonstrated his great talent and bravery by prevailing on such a demanding and special track like Laguna Seca.

81

Located in the northeast of Qatar, there is a circuit that is 5,400 meters long and consists of 16 corners, but this is not what's interesting about it.

This circuit is the only one that takes place at night, as during the day, the track reaches 45 degrees Celsius, making it impossible to race for both the riders and the machines.

Its construction was in record time, as the circuit was delivered in 10 months.

More than 1,000 people worked there and the evaluation of the track was carried out by the MotoGP Safety Commission, which includes riders such as Valentino Rossi, Sete Gibernau, Kenny Roberts Jr., and Nobuatsu Aoki.

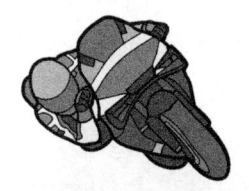

82

Valentino Rossi is known for his great personality and sense of humor both on and off the track.

In addition to being a very talented rider, he has been the protagonist of some jokes and funny moments that have remained in the memory of the fans.

Among the most remembered moments is the one you mention, when Rossi walked around the circuit in his swimsuit after a race due to the heat.

His chicken prank is also famous, where he appeared with a chicken on his head on the podium to promote a friend's poultry shop.

Additionally, Rossi has also played other pranks, such as when he dressed up as Totti, the famous Italian footballer, or when he raced on the Misano circuit with a motorcycle decorated with Simpsons cartoons.

Regarding his character, Rossi is known for being very competitive and having a strong temper, especially when things don't go his way on the track.

However, he is also a very respected and beloved rider by his rivals and fans, and has shown great humility and sportsmanship on numerous occasions.

83

Colin Edwards is a former American MotoGP rider who competed in the premier class for 11 seasons, from 2003 to 2014.

Known for his straightforward and unfiltered style, he was a very popular figure in the MotoGP paddock.

He made a very peculiar comment in the context of a race where Edwards had trouble with his bike, which led him to express his frustration in a blunt interview with the press.

"My bike is a piece of shit. It's better than saying it fucked me".

The phrase became famous for its frankness and the humorous tone Edwards gave to the situation, which earned him the respect and sympathy of many fans.

Throughout his career, Edwards achieved two victories in MotoGP and 12 podiums, as well as a World Superbike title before making the jump to the premier class.

After retiring from competition, he has continued to be involved in the world of motorbikes as a commentator and ambassador for various brands.

84

The 2010 Malaysian Grand Prix was an exciting race for Jorge Lorenzo, who achieved victory and his second world championship in the MotoGP category.

After crossing the finish line, the Spanish rider decided to take a victory lap with a Spanish flag he had taken from one of his mechanics.

However, during the lap, the flag got tangled in the rear wheel of the bike, causing it to be shredded and forcing Lorenzo to stop the bike to free it.

Despite the embarrassing situation, Lorenzo didn't lose heart and continued his victory lap with the Spanish flag in his hand, greeting fans in the stands of the Sepang circuit.

Later, he apologized for what happened and assured that it was an accident.

The image of Lorenzo with the Spanish flag in his hand and the shredded flag in the rear wheel of his bike became one of the most iconic of his career.

85

The tobacco brand Marlboro has been a long-time presence in the MotoGP world championship.

Wayne Rainey's Yamaha, which led him to the 500cc title on three occasions (1990, 1991, and 1992), displayed the firm's logo and name on the sides, in full view of the world.

Later, Ducati also incorporated it when it made its debut in the championship back in 2003.

With the continuous prohibitions on tobacco advertising by various countries around the world, its exposure has plummeted to the point of disappearing its identity in favor of one of its campaigns: Mission Winnow.

Since 2019, this initiative that seeks a smoke-free future accompanies the red bikes of Borgo Panigale at every Grand Prix.

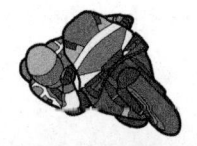

86

Lucky Strike.

It is a cigarette brand that has sponsored MotoGP teams on several occasions.

In the case of Suzuki, the brand sponsored the official team for several years, including the period when Kevin Schwantz won the 500cc world championship in 1993.

Schwantz's bike that year, the Suzuki RGV500, became a legend of MotoGP, especially for the thrilling battles he had with his teammate and rival Wayne Rainey.

The combination of the bike's design, with the colors and brand image of Lucky Strike, was very popular among motorcycle racing fans.

However, in 2000, tobacco advertising was banned in many countries, including Spain where several MotoGP races are held, and Lucky Strike withdrew from sponsoring the Suzuki team.

87

Movistar, the Spanish telecommunications giant, was heavily involved in motorcycle racing during its time with MotoGP.

To start with, it sponsored the promotion championship that led Dani Pedrosa to fulfill his dream and, later on, financially backed different teams in the three categories.

Therefore, it is one of the ones that has undoubtedly tasted the most success.

It accompanied the number 26 towards his three world titles achieved in 125 and 250cc with Honda, did the same with Kenny Roberts Jr in 500cc with Suzuki, and Jorge Lorenzo in 2015 when he was with Yamaha and embarked on competitive teams, such as Gresini, which saw the best of Sete Gibernau, or Aspar Aprilia, with which Fonsi Nieto and Toni Elías fought for the quarter-liter title.

It bid farewell to the world championship in 2018 when it stopped broadcasting the races on television, and it did so by sponsoring Yamaha.

88

Repsol has been one of the main players in MotoGP since 1995, when it became the main sponsor of the official Honda team.

Its arrival coincided with a period of great success for the Golden Wing, especially with the consecutive titles won by Mick Doohan between 1995 and 1998, and the title won by Álex Crivillé the following year in 1999.

Previously, Repsol had played a more secondary role with other teams.

The arrival of Valentino Rossi to the team added to the company's list of achievements, as he continued the legacy of the Australian and the Spaniard in 2002 and 2003 with the first two championships in the history of the MotoGP category.

Marc Márquez is the latest rider to link his name to Repsol with great joy, having won six titles among the best (2013, 2014, 2016, 2017, 2018, and 2019).

In addition, Repsol also accompanied Dani Pedrosa to his three championships and was also associated with Toni Elías and Fonsi Nieto at the same time as Movistar under the name Telefónica Movistar.

89

Car brands also invest part of their advertising in the world of two wheels.

Fiat did so with the official Yamaha team between 2007 and 2010, contributing a great touch of white to the Yamaha M1s that crowned Valentino Rossi in 2008 and 2009, and Jorge Lorenzo in 2010.

Their role as main sponsor was brief compared to others, but successful.

It could not have had better promotion than the duel between the Italian and the Spanish during the 2009 Catalan Grand Prix at Montmeló, which was won by Il Dottore.

However, with Rossi's departure to Ducati, Fiat put an end to its marriage with the tuning fork brand.

However, its subsidiary Abarth had a place on the blue bikes when Rossi returned to the team, although in a very discreet location on both sides of the top fairing when Movistar became the main sponsor.

90

Red Bull, the energy drink, has devoted a great deal of effort to the championship, both by supporting riders and teams.

Marc Marquez, Dani Pedrosa, and Andrea Dovizioso are just a few who rely on its benefits to compete in a race just before it starts and have to focus on what's ahead at over 300 kilometers per hour.

In the 90s, it was with Yamaha and celebrated some victories with Regis Laconi and Gary McCoy.

However, with KTM's appearance in the championship, it gained a lot of prominence in teams that rode Austrian factory bikes.

Especially in the categories of 125 cc, 250 cc, and later Moto2, before having an official team among the best since 2017.

The values of this brand and the characteristics of motorcycling go hand in hand, so Red Bull promises to be here for a long time.

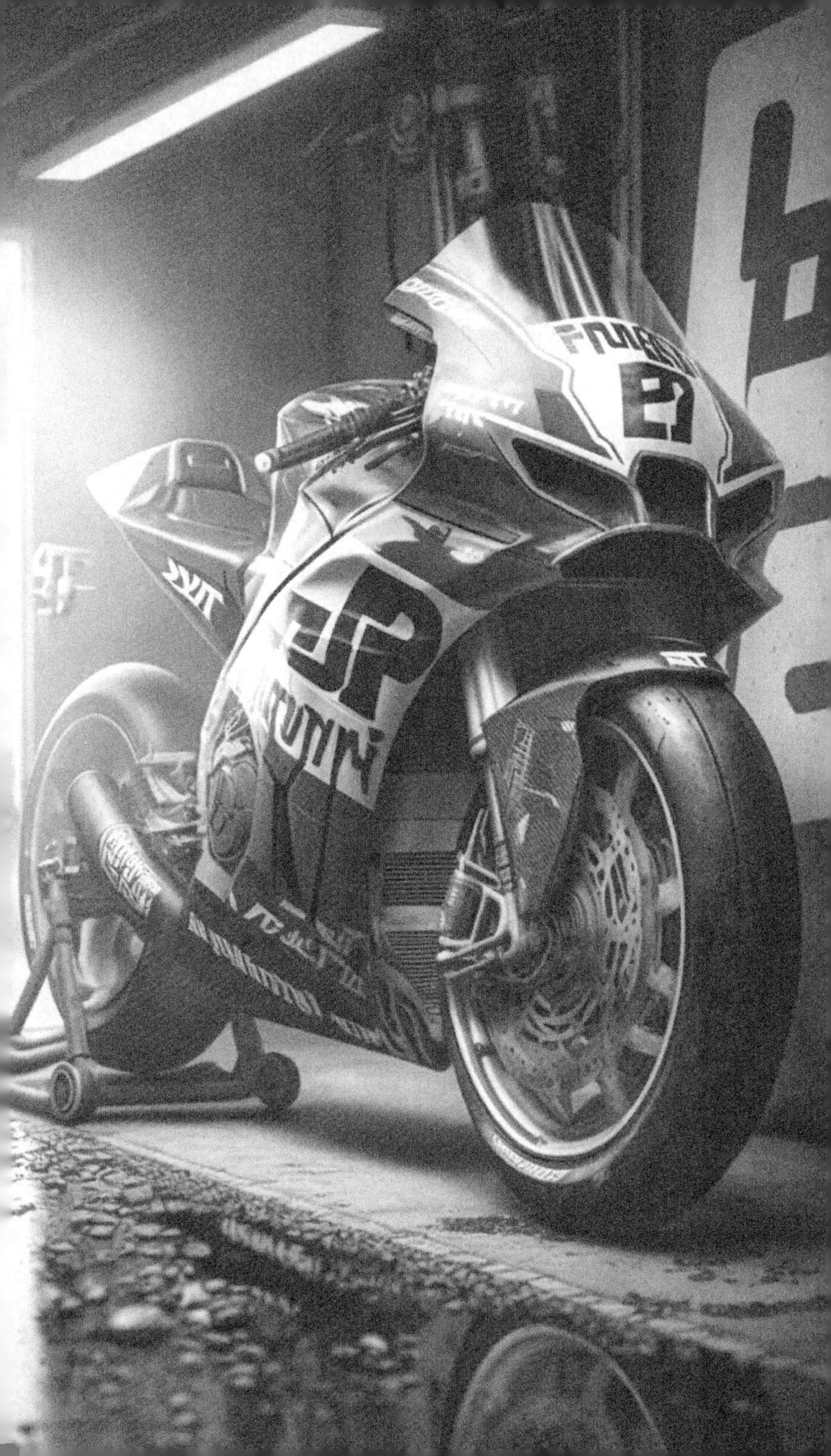

91

Another tobacco brand that played an important role in the MotoGP world championship was Fortuna.

In 250 cc, it dressed Honda and Aprilia, accompanying Jorge Lorenzo in his 2 titles won in the quarter-liter class (2006 and 2007).

In 500 cc, they previously lived alongside Alberto Puig for his first world victory in Jerez (1995), and in MotoGP, they supported both Yamaha and Honda.

In the premier class, they supported the satellite team of the tuning fork brand and that of the golden wing, when the latter was under the command of Fausto Gresini.

However, they never won a championship despite celebrating victories with Marco Melandri and that of Toni Elias in Estoril during 2006, the last season they were in the championship due to the reasons we mentioned earlier with tobacco companies.

92

Gauloises, the French tobacco brand, also played an important role during their stay in the motorcycle world championship.

In 1984, they saw their compatriot Christian Sarron become the 250cc champion, a glory that took a long time to taste on a large scale again.

And with the arrival of Valentino Rossi at Yamaha and the titles in 2004 and 2005, their advertising as the main sponsor was unbeatable.

Considering that they had jumped to the 500cc with Tech3, previously the satellite team of the Japanese, they probably could not even imagine reaching the highest possible success.

The truth is that they left on a high note, as they were replaced by a competitor, Camel, to dress Rossi and his teammate Colin Edwards in yellow in 2006.

93

The main competition for Red Bull, Monster, has been gaining prominence little by little in the championship: first supporting riders and later teams.

Valentino Rossi was the first big star of the championship to trust it when preparing for races.

Later, it decorated the bikes of Yamaha Tech3 and now does the same with those of the official team of the tuning forks.

It entered the main structure in 2019 after the departure of Movistar, and its great success is very recent thanks to the MotoGP title achieved by Fabio Quartararo in 2021.

It should be noted that when Valentino Rossi went to Ducati, it also had visibility thanks to its presence on Il Dottore's caps.

94

Monster Energy Yamaha: Fabio Quartararo (20) and Franco Morbidelli (21).

The official Yamaha team reunited the Frenchman and reigning champion, Fabio Quartararo, with the Italo-Brazilian Franco Morbidelli, as they had done in their satellite formation a few years ago.

Both had a mixed season in 2021, as while one dominated the championship with an iron fist, the other wandered around the mid-low zone aimlessly.

They did not shine as much as others in the pre-season tests, but we are talking about the team that defends the riders' crown.

They performed very well together in the Petronas team during 2019 and 2020, achieving great results.

In fact, Morbidelli was the runner-up in 2020.

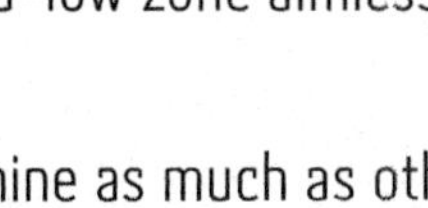

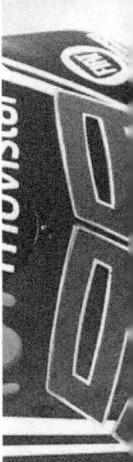

95

Davide Tardozzi is a former motorcycle racer and currently the team manager of BMW Motorrad in the World Superbike Championship.

Born in Italy in 1959, Tardozzi began his motorcycle racing career in the 1980s, competing in both the 250cc and 500cc categories of the Motorcycle World Championship.

Throughout his career, Tardozzi achieved several notable successes on the track, including 2 Grand Prix victories and multiple podium finishes in both categories.

After retiring as a rider in 1991, Tardozzi worked as a television commentator and as a team manager in the World Superbike Championship.

In 2007, Tardozzi joined the BMW Motorrad team in the World Superbike Championship, first as the sporting director and later as the team manager.

Under his leadership, the team has achieved several notable successes, including the World Superbike Championship in 2010 and 2012, and multiple race wins and podiums in subsequent seasons.

Tardozzi is known for his disciplined and methodical approach to the sport, and for his ability to build and lead successful teams.

He is also recognized for his skill in developing competitive motorcycles and maximizing the performance of riders on the track.

96

Julián Simón is a retired Spanish motorcycle racer who has been very successful in his career as a personal trainer for MotoGP riders.

Born in Valencia on April 3, 1987, Simón began his professional racing career in 2002, competing in the 125cc category of the MotoGP World Championship.

Throughout his career, Simón achieved several notable successes on the track, including 7 Grand Prix victories and the Moto2 World Championship in 2009.

After retiring as a rider in 2017, he decided to pursue his passion for the sport by working as a personal trainer for MotoGP riders.

Simón has worked with several riders in his career as a trainer, including Pol Espargaró and Álex Rins.

His approach focuses on improving the technique and physical endurance of riders, as well as the mental and emotional preparation to compete at the highest level.

Simón is known for his personalized and detailed approach to training riders, adapting his methods to the specific needs of each individual.

He also works closely with teams to help develop more competitive motorcycles.

97

Alberto Puig.

He is one of the most important figures in the world of motorcycling, known for his success as a motorcycle racer and his role as a coach and team manager in MotoGP.

Born on January 16, 1967 in Barcelona, Spain, Puig started his career in the world of motorcycling as a rider.

He competed in several categories, including 125cc, 250cc, and 500cc, and won the 250cc World Championship in 1995.

After retiring as a rider in 1997, Puig became a coach and team manager in MotoGP.

He has worked with various teams and riders, including the Honda team, where he currently holds the position of Team Manager for the Repsol Honda team.

Puig is known for his rigorous and demanding approach in training and physical preparation of riders and has helped many riders reach their full potential on the track.

He has worked with some of the most successful riders in the history of MotoGP, including Dani Pedrosa, Casey Stoner, and Marc Marquez, who has won several world championships under Puig's tutelage.

In addition to his work in the world of motorcycling, Puig is also a successful entrepreneur.

He is the founder and owner of Puig Racing, a company that manufactures high-quality parts for competition motorcycles.

98

Ramon Forcada is a famous Spanish motorcycle engineer and coach.

He is widely recognized for his expertise and skills in motorcycle development, as well as his ability to train riders and help them reach their full potential on the track.

Forcada began his career in the world of motorcycle racing in the 1980s as a mechanic with the Yamaha team, and quickly rose through the ranks to become the chief engineer.

He has worked with several successful riders, including Jorge Lorenzo, Álex Rins, Pol Espargaró, Bradley Smith, Tito Rabat, Toni Elías, among others.

In his career as a coach and team manager, Forcada has been instrumental in the success of several teams and riders.

He has helped develop race-winning motorcycles and worked to maximize riders' performance on the track.

One of his greatest achievements as a coach was his work with Jorge Lorenzo, who won several MotoGP world championships under his tutelage.

Forcada has also worked with Álex Rins, whom he has helped become a frequent contender in the MotoGP category.

Forcada is known for his attention to detail and his focus on motorcycle mechanics and performance.

He is also recognized for his ability to motivate riders and help them develop their confidence on the track.

99

Wilco Zeelenberg.

He is a former Dutch motorcycle racer who has worked as a coach for several riders, including Maverick Viñales.

Zeelenberg had a successful career in motorcycle racing, competing in the 250cc category of the Motorcycle World Championship for several years.

In total, he won 14 races and obtained 44 podiums in his career in the World Championship.

After retiring as a rider, Zeelenberg began working as a coach for riders.

In 2010, he started working as a sports director for the Yamaha World Supersport team.

In 2013, he joined the Yamaha MotoGP team as a coach for Jorge Lorenzo and helped the Spanish rider win two world titles in 2013 and 2015.

In 2017, Zeelenberg began working as a coach for Maverick Viñales on the Yamaha MotoGP team.

Since then, he has been part of Viñales' team and has helped the Spanish rider improve his performance on the track.

Zeelenberg is known for being a coach focused on details and has worked closely with Viñales to improve his technique and race strategy.

100

Carlo Pernat.

He is a well-known Italian motorcycle coach, who has worked with some of Italy's most prominent riders, including Loris Capirossi, Marco Melandri, Andrea Iannone, Danilo Petrucci, Andrea Dovizioso, Valentino Rossi, and many others.

Born in 1949 in the Italian city of Milan, Pernat began his career in the world of motorcycle racing as a mechanic for the Garelli team, where he worked with Italian rider Paolo Pileri in the 1980s.

Pernat later became the director of the Aprilia racing team, where he worked with several renowned Italian riders, including Loris Capirossi and Valentino Rossi.

Pernat is known for his unique and effective coaching style, which focuses on motivating riders and their ability to focus on racing and riding techniques.

Pernat believes that self-confidence and confidence in one's team are essential to success in the world of motorcycle racing, and works intensely with his riders to help them develop their confidence and skills on the track.

In 1997, Pernat was the director of the Aprilia Racing team, which won the 250cc World Championship with Loris Capirossi.

Since then, he has worked as a personal coach for several Italian riders and has been recognized as one of the most influential and successful coaches in the world of Italian motorcycle racing.

101

Luca Cadalora.

He is a former Italian motorcycle racer,
born on February 17th, 1963 in Modena.

He is considered one of the most talented riders of his era
and has been an important figure in the world of
motorcycle racing since his debut in 1983.

Throughout his career, Cadalora has achieved several notable
successes on the track, including the 250cc World
Championship in 1991, 1992, and 1993,
and 5 Grand Prix victories.

After retiring from racing in 1996, he became
a personal coach for MotoGP riders.

Cadalora has worked with several successful riders in
his coaching career, including Andrea Dovizioso
and Franco Morbidelli.

His focus is on improving riders' technique and physical
endurance, as well as mental and emotional
preparation to compete at the highest level.

Cadalora is known for his personalized and detailed approach
to rider coaching, adapting his methods to the
specific needs of each individual.

He also works closely with teams to help develop
more competitive motorcycles.

If you have enjoyed the curiosities of MotoGP presented in this book, we would like to ask you to share a review on Amazon.

Your opinion is very valuable to us and to other MotoGP enthusiasts who are looking to be entertained and learn new knowledge about this sport.

We understand that leaving a comment can be a tedious process, but we kindly ask you to take a few minutes of your time to share your thoughts and opinions with us.

Your support is very important to us and it helps us continue creating quality content for fans of this incredible sport.

We appreciate your support and hope that you have enjoyed reading our book as much as we enjoyed writing it.

Thank you for sharing your experience with us!

★ ★ ★ ★ ★

Printed in Great Britain
by Amazon